Betty Crocker
PICTURE COOKBOOK

Hors d'Oeuvres and Party Snacks

🦉 GOLDEN PRESS/NEW YORK
Western Publishing Company, Inc.,
Racine, Wisconsin

CONTENTS

Hearty Party Snacks

Mix cornstarch and ½ cup of the pizza sauce; stir in the remaining pizza sauce.

Stir the cheese cubes into hot mixture, ½ cup at a time, until the cheese is melted.

Pizza Fondue

2 tablespoons cornstarch
2 cans (10½ ounces each) pizza sauce with cheese
¼ pound pepperoni, finely chopped
1 tablespoon instant minced onion
1 teaspoon dried oregano leaves
1 package (16 ounces) pasteurized process cheese food, cut into ½-inch cubes
1 tablespoon snipped parsley
3 or 4 drops red pepper sauce
Vegetable Dippers (below)

Mix cornstarch and ½ cup of the pizza sauce in 2-quart saucepan; stir in remaining pizza sauce. Add pepperoni, onion and oregano. Heat to boiling, stirring constantly. Boil and stir 1 minute; remove from heat. Stir in cheese, ½ cup at a time, until melted. Stir in parsley and pepper sauce. Pour into fondue pot to keep warm. Your guests can spear Vegetable Dippers and swirl them in fondue.
8 SERVINGS.

VEGETABLE DIPPERS
Serve the following in small bowls: 1 cup cherry tomatoes, 1 green pepper, cut into pieces, 8 breadsticks, cut into 1-inch pieces, and ½ cup fresh mushroom halves or 1 can (4 ounces) button mushrooms, drained.

Curried Fritter Fondue

Curry Batter (right)
Vegetable oil
1 medium apple, cut into ½-inch cubes
1 medium pear, cut into ½-inch cubes
Lemon juice
2 ounces Gouda, Edam or Provolone cheese,
cut into bite-size pieces
½ cup maraschino cherries, well drained
1 cup pecan halves
5 large marshmallows, cut in half
Powdered sugar

Prepare Curry Batter. Heat oil (2 inches) to 375° in metal fondue pot. Dip apple and pear cubes into lemon juice. Pat dry and arrange on tray with cheese, cherries, pecans and marshmallows.

Have your guests spear cheese, fruit, pecans or marshmallows with color-coded fondue forks, dip them into Curry Batter and then into the hot oil about 1 minute. Fritters should be drained on paper towels or paper napkins, then dipped in sugar.　4 TO 6 SERVINGS.

CURRY BATTER

　1　egg
⅓　cup milk
　1　cup biscuit baking mix
　2　tablespoons white cornmeal
½　teaspoon curry powder
⅛　teaspoon salt

Beat egg slightly; stir in milk. Stir in remaining ingredients. Add more milk if batter becomes too thick.

Heat oil in fondue pot and arrange fruit, cheese, pecans and marshmallows on tray.

Have your guests spear the dippers, dip them into Curry Batter and then into hot oil.

Puffs with Honey-Butter Dip

3 eggs
1 carton (8 ounces) unflavored yogurt
3 tablespoons butter or margarine, softened
2 cups all-purpose flour*
2 teaspoons baking powder
1 teaspoon baking soda
½ teaspoon ground nutmeg
¼ teaspoon salt
  Vegetable oil
  Honey-Butter Dip (below)

Beat eggs in large mixer bowl on high speed until lemon colored, about 3 minutes. Beat in yogurt and butter on low speed. Add flour, baking powder, baking soda, nutmeg and salt; beat in on low speed.

Heat oil (2 to 3 inches) to 360° in deep fat fryer or 3-quart saucepan. Drop dough by level teaspoonfuls into oil. Fry until light brown, about 2 minutes; drain. Serve with Honey-Butter Dip.   4 DOZEN PUFFS.

*If using self-rising flour, omit baking powder and salt.

HONEY-BUTTER DIP
Beat ¼ cup butter or margarine, softened, and ¼ cup honey in small mixer bowl until light and fluffy.

Drop dough by level teaspoonfuls into the hot oil.

Fry puffs until light brown; drain on paper towels.

Meatballs and Jalapeño Dip

    2 pounds ground beef
    2 eggs
 ⅔ cup dry bread crumbs
    1 medium onion, chopped (about ½ cup)
 ½ cup milk
 ¼ cup toasted sesame seed
 ¼ cup snipped parsley
    2 teaspoons Worcestershire sauce
1½ teaspoons salt
    1 teaspoon prepared horseradish
 ¼ teaspoon pepper
    Jalapeño Dip (right)

Heat oven to 400°. Mix all ingredients except Jalapeño Dip. Shape ground beef mixture by spoonfuls into 1¼-inch balls. (For easy shaping, dip hands in cold water from time to time.) Place meatballs in 2 ungreased baking pans, 13x9x2 or 15½x10½x1 inch. Bake uncovered until light brown, about 20 minutes; drain. Serve with Jalapeño Dip.
7 TO 9 DOZEN MEATBALLS.

Toast the sesame seed in 350° oven until golden, about 10 minutes, stirring occasionally.

Remove stems, seeds and membrane from the jalapeño chili peppers; chop peppers.

Cut up cheese spread; cook and stir until melted.

Stir the peppers and tomato into cheese mixture.

JALAPEÑO DIP

2 jalapeño chili peppers, drained
2 tablespoons butter or margarine
1 package (16 ounces) pasteurized process
   cheese spread, cut up
1 medium tomato, peeled and chopped (about
   ¾ cup)

Remove stems, seeds and membrane from peppers; chop peppers. Heat butter in 1-quart saucepan over low heat until melted. Stir in cheese; cook and stir until cheese is melted. Stir peppers and tomato into cheese mixture; heat until tomato is hot.

To shred a firm to hard cheese such as Cheddar, use the medium-coarse holes of a grater.

For easy mixing or blending, cream cheese should first be softened to room temperature.

Cheese Spreads

SESAME-CHEDDAR SPREAD

  2 cups shredded sharp Cheddar cheese,
     (about 8 ounces)
  2 packages (3 ounces each) cream cheese
  ¼ cup light cream or milk
  ¼ cup toasted sesame seed
  1 teaspoon soy sauce
  ½ teaspoon seasoned salt

Mix all ingredients until smooth.

HAM-CAMEMBERT SPREAD

  8 ounces Camembert cheese (room
     temperature)
  ½ cup butter or margarine, softened
  ¼ cup light cream or milk
  1 cup finely chopped sliced smoked ham
     (about 6 ounces)
  2 tablespoons finely chopped green onion
  ½ teaspoon celery seed

Blend cheese, butter and cream until smooth. Stir in remaining ingredients.

BLUE CHEESE-WALNUT SPREAD

  2 jars (5 ounces each) pasteurized
     Neufchâtel cheese spread with pimiento
  8 ounces blue cheese, crumbled
  2 packages (3 ounces each) cream cheese
  ½ cup finely chopped walnuts

Blend cheeses until smooth; stir in walnuts.

Note: Pack cheese spreads in crocks or in glass or plastic
containers. Cover and refrigerate at least 24 hours but no
longer than 2 weeks. Remove from refrigerator about 1
hour before serving.   EACH SPREAD MAKES ABOUT 2 CUPS.

Shape dough into 6 balls; roll each into thin 9-inch square.

Cut into 3-inch squares and place on baking sheet; bake.

Graham Wafers with Spreads

- 1 cup graham or whole wheat flour
- 1 cup all-purpose flour*
- 1 cup yellow cornmeal
- 3 tablespoons sugar
- 1¼ teaspoons baking soda
- 1 teaspoon salt
- 1 cup buttermilk
- ¼ cup vegetable oil
  Deviled Ham Spread, Honey Spread and
  Sesame Spread (right)

Heat oven to 350°. Mix flours, cornmeal, sugar, baking soda and salt. Stir in buttermilk and oil. Shape dough into 6 balls. Roll each ball into very thin 9-inch square on floured cloth-covered board. Cut into 3-inch squares. (Dough can be rerolled.) Place squares on ungreased baking sheet. Bake until crisp and golden, 8 to 10 minutes. Serve with spreads. ABOUT 6 DOZEN WAFERS.

DEVILED HAM SPREAD

Mix 1 can (4½ ounces) deviled ham, 1 package (3 ounces) cream cheese, softened, 1 tablespoon mayonnaise or salad dressing and 1 teaspoon finely chopped green onion. Refrigerate until serving time.

HONEY SPREAD

Beat 1 package (3 ounces) cream cheese, softened, and 2 tablespoons honey until thoroughly blended.

SESAME SPREAD

Mix ½ cup butter or margarine, softened, and 2 tablespoons toasted sesame seed.

Honeydew Cups and Nibbles

Pare 1 chilled medium honeydew melon and cut into cubes or balls. Spoon melon into 6 shallow stemmed glasses. Pour 2 tablespoons chilled white wine (Rhine or sauterne) on melon in each glass. Sprinkle each serving with 1 tablespoon shredded Swiss cheese.   6 SERVINGS.

CHEESE TOMATO

Mix 1 package (3 ounces) cream cheese, softened, and ¼ teaspoon each smoky salt and instant minced onion. Cover and refrigerate 1 hour. Shape mixture to resemble tomato as pictured; coat with paprika. Place parsley sprig on top for stem. Serve with crackers.   4 TO 6 SERVINGS.

GUACAMOLE CHEESE DIP

1 bottle (8 ounces) green goddess salad
    dressing, chilled
1 can (7¾ ounces) frozen avocado dip,
    thawed in refrigerator
2 cans (4½ ounces each) deveined tiny
    shrimp, rinsed, drained and chilled
1 cup shredded Swiss or taco-flavored cheese
    (about 4 ounces)
    Few drops red pepper sauce (optional)
1 cup uncooked small broccoli flowerets
    Crackers

Mix salad dressing, avocado dip, shrimp, cheese and red pepper sauce. Serve immediately with broccoli flowerets and crackers.   ABOUT 3½ CUPS DIP.

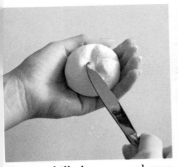

Shape chilled cream cheese mixture into the shape of a tomato with knife.

Coat with paprika; add parsley sprig for a stem. Repeat recipe for more tomatoes.

Garden Cheesecake

2½ cups crushed cheese snack crackers
 ½ cup butter or margarine, melted
 1 package (8 ounces) cream cheese,
   softened
 1 carton (8 ounces) unflavored yogurt
 ½ cup pimiento-stuffed olives
 1 medium green pepper, cut into large
   pieces
 1 small onion, cut into fourths
 1 medium stalk celery, cut into 1-inch
   pieces
 1 teaspoon salt
 1 teaspoon Worcestershire sauce
 ¼ teaspoon paprika
   Dash of red pepper sauce
   Assorted raw vegetables

Mix cracker crumbs and butter. Reserve half of the crumb mixture. Press remaining crumb mixture firmly and evenly in bottom of ungreased 9-inch springform pan.

Place cheese and yogurt in blender container. Cover and blend on low speed just until smooth. Add olives, green pepper pieces, onion, celery pieces, salt, Worcestershire sauce, paprika and pepper sauce. Blend on low speed just until vegetables are finely chopped. Pour over crumb base. Sprinkle with reserved crumbs. Refrigerate 24 hours before serving. Serve with raw vegetables.   16 SERVINGS.

For best results, crush only about ⅓ of the cheese snack crackers at a time in blender.

Add seasonings to the cheese mixture and vegetables in blender; blend on low speed.

Pour vegetable mixture over crumb base in springform pan.

Sprinkle with the reserved crumbs; refrigerate 24 hours.

Shape cheese-chicken mixture into a log, 8x2 inches.

Cut the green pepper rings to make strips for log.

Place the strips diagonally across log, dividing evenly.

Sprinkle with sesame seed, onion, olives and pimiento.

Festive Chicken Salad Log

1 package (8 ounces) cream cheese, softened
¼ cup mayonnaise or salad dressing
2 tablespoons lemon juice
½ teaspoon salt
¼ teaspoon ground ginger
⅛ teaspoon pepper
4 drops red pepper sauce
2 cups finely cut-up cooked chicken
2 hard-cooked eggs, chopped
¼ cup sliced green onions (2 to 3 medium)
3 green pepper rings
1 tablespoon toasted sesame seed
3 tablespoons chopped green onion or green
    pepper
3 tablespoons chopped pitted ripe olives
3 tablespoons chopped pimiento, drained
    Crackers or bread rounds

Mix cheese, mayonnaise, lemon juice, salt, ginger, pepper and pepper sauce. Stir in chicken, eggs and ¼ cup onions. Shape into log, 8x2 inches. Wrap in plastic wrap; refrigerate until firm, about 4 hours.

Cut green pepper rings to make strips. Place strips diagonally across log, dividing log into fourths as pictured. Sprinkle sesame seed on 1 section. Repeat with 3 tablespoons onion, the olives and pimiento on remaining sections. Serve with crackers.   10 TO 12 SERVINGS.

Beef Empanadas

1 pound ground beef
1 small onion, chopped (about ¼ cup)
1 medium potato, finely chopped (about ½ cup)
1 can (8½ ounces) peas and carrots, drained (reserve liquid)
1 package (about 1 ounce) mushroom gravy mix
1 package (22 ounces) pie crust mix
Paprika

Cook and stir ground beef and onion in 10-inch skillet until beef is light brown and onion is tender; drain. Stir in potato, peas and carrots and gravy mix. Add enough water to reserved vegetable liquid to measure 1 cup; stir into beef mixture in skillet. Heat to boiling; reduce heat. Simmer uncovered, stirring occasionally, 1 minute. Cool.

Heat oven to 400°. Prepare pastry for 2 Two-Crust Pies as directed on pie crust mix package except—after rolling pastry, cut into 3-inch rounds. Place rounds on ungreased baking sheets.

Spoon scant tablespoon beef mixture onto half of each round. Fold pastry over filling as pictured; seal with fork. Sprinkle with paprika. Bake until light brown, about 15 minutes. (Empanadas can be baked ahead and frozen up to 3 weeks. Fifteen minutes before serving, place frozen empanadas on ungreased baking sheet and heat in 400° oven 15 minutes.)   ABOUT 5 DOZEN APPETIZERS.

Simmer beef mixture, stirring occasionally, 1 minute.

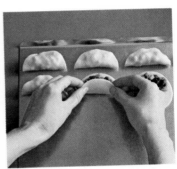
Fold pastry rounds over beef mixture; seal with fork.

Beef Wrap-ups

½ pound ground beef
1 small onion, chopped (about ¼ cup)
2 tablespoons grated American cheese food
¼ teaspoon salt
¼ teaspoon garlic salt
1 egg, separated
1 cup all-purpose flour*
⅓ cup water
½ teaspoon salt
¼ teaspoon paprika
Vegetable oil or shortening

Mix ground beef, onion, cheese, ¼ teaspoon salt, the garlic salt and egg white; reserve. Mix flour, egg yolk, water, ½ teaspoon salt and the paprika until a soft dough forms. Knead on floured surface until dough is elastic, about 2 minutes. Divide dough in half. Roll half into 12-inch square about 1/16 inch thick; cut into 2-inch squares.

Fill each square with scant teaspoon beef mixture. Moisten edges of squares; fold into triangles. Pinch edges together. Repeat with remaining dough. Heat oil (1 inch) to 400° in 10-inch skillet. Fry wrap-ups until golden, about 45 seconds; drain. Serve hot or cold.   6 DOZEN APPETIZERS.

*Do not use self-rising flour in this recipe.

Cut dough into squares.

Dot with beef mixture.

Moisten, fold and pinch.

Fry until golden brown.

Runzas

- 1 pound ground beef
- 4 cups shredded cabbage
- ¼ cup water
- 1 small onion, chopped (about ¼ cup)
- 1 teaspoon salt
- ½ teaspoon caraway seed
- ⅛ teaspoon pepper
  Yeast Roll Dough (right)

Cook and stir ground beef until light brown; drain. Stir in cabbage, water, onion, salt, caraway seed and pepper. Heat to boiling; reduce heat. Cover and simmer until cabbage is tender, about 10 minutes. Prepare Yeast Roll Dough; roll into rectangle, 20x15 inches, about ¼ inch thick. Cut into 3-inch circles; spoon beef mixture onto center of each circle. Bring side to center and pinch dough to seal as pictured. Place on greased baking sheet. Let rise in warm place until double, about 1 hour. Heat oven to 375°. Bake until golden, about 18 minutes.   2½ DOZEN RUNZAS.

YEAST ROLL DOUGH

2 packages active dry yeast
¾ cup warm water (105 to 115°)
1¼ cups buttermilk
¼ cup shortening
2 tablespoons sugar
2 teaspoons baking powder
2 teaspoons salt
4½ to 5 cups all-purpose flour

Dissolve yeast in warm water in large mixer bowl. Add buttermilk, shortening, sugar, baking powder, salt and 2½ cups of the flour. Blend on low speed, scraping bowl constantly, 30 seconds. Beat on medium speed, scraping bowl occasionally, 2 minutes. Stir in enough remaining flour to make dough easy to handle. Turn dough onto well-floured surface; knead 5 minutes.

Roll dough into a rectangle and cut into 3-inch circles.

Spoon rounded tablespoon of beef mixture onto centers.

Bring edge to center, stretching to cover; pinch to seal and place on baking sheet.

For last minute reheating of baked Runzas, cover and heat in 350° oven 20 minutes.

Place 3 tablespoons filling in center of each circle.

Bring 2 edges of circle together; pinch edges to seal.

Meat Turnovers

- **1 package active dry yeast**
- **1 cup warm water (105 to 115°)**
- **1 tablespoon sugar**
- **1 tablespoon vegetable oil**
- **½ teaspoon salt**
- **2 to 2½ cups all-purpose flour**
  Chopped Liver Filling (right)

Dissolve yeast in warm water. Stir in sugar, oil, salt and enough flour to make dough easy to handle; turn onto floured surface. Knead until smooth and elastic, about 5 minutes. Place in greased bowl; turn greased side up. Cover; let rise until double, about 1 hour. Prepare filling.

Punch down dough; divide into 10 parts. Roll into 5-inch circles. Fill circles as pictured. Place seam sides down on greased baking sheets. Cover with damp towel. Let rise until double, about 1 hour. Heat oven to 375°. Bake until light brown, 20 to 23 minutes.   10 TURNOVERS.

28

CHOPPED LIVER FILLING

- 5 ounces mushrooms, chopped
- 1 small onion, chopped (about ¼ cup)
- 1 clove garlic, crushed
- ¼ cup vegetable oil
- ½ pound chicken livers
- 1 tablespoon snipped parsley
- 1 teaspoon salt
- ½ teaspoon dried dill weed
- ⅛ teaspoon pepper
- 1 hard-cooked egg, finely chopped

Cook and stir mushrooms, onion and garlic in half of the oil until onion is tender; remove from pan. Cook and stir livers in remaining oil 10 minutes. Chop livers; mix with mushroom mixture and remaining ingredients.

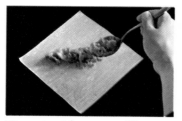

Place 3 tablespoons filling on each egg roll wrapper.

Fold the lower corner of the wrapper up over the filling.

Fold in sides, forming an envelope; moisten top corner.

Roll up from bottom; seal. Fry sealed sides down first.

Pork Egg Rolls

3 tablespoons soy sauce
2 tablespoons dry sherry
1 teaspoon salt
1 teaspoon sugar
¼ teaspoon pepper
1 pound pork boneless steak, cut into
   1x¼-inch pieces
   Vegetable oil
3 cups finely shredded cabbage
1 can (8½ ounces) bamboo shoots, drained
   and chopped
1 can (4½ ounces) mushrooms stems and
   pieces, drained
6 medium green onions, sliced
¼ teaspoon salt
1 tablespoon cornstarch
1 pound egg roll wrapper skins (16 to 18)

Mix soy sauce, sherry, 1 teaspoon salt, the sugar and pepper; pour on pork pieces. Let stand, stirring occasionally, 5 minutes. Drain well, reserving marinade. Cook and stir pork in 1 tablespoon oil in 10-inch skillet until light brown, about 4 minutes. Remove pork to large bowl.

Stir-fry cabbage, bamboo shoots, mushrooms and onions in 1 tablespoon oil in same skillet 2 minutes. Sprinkle with ¼ teaspoon salt. Add to pork. Heat cornstarch and marinade to boiling in skillet, stirring constantly. Boil and stir 1 minute. Return pork and vegetables to skillet. Boil and stir 1 minute; cool 5 minutes.

Heat oil (1½ to 1¾ inches) to 400° in deep fat fryer or electric skillet. Place filling on each wrapper; fold as pictured. Fry 4 at a time, sealed sides down first, until brown, 2 minutes on each side; drain.   16 TO 18 EGG ROLLS.

Egg rolls refer to paper-thin Oriental "envelopes" that hold a variety of tasty fillings.

Fruit Kabobs

2 cans (11 ounces each) mandarin orange
    segments and pineapple tidbits, drained
1 pound green grapes
1 large cucumber, cut up
½ cup mint-flavored apple jelly
3 tablespoons water
½ teaspoon poppy seed

Alternate fruit and cucumber on 5-inch skewers. Heat jelly until melted; stir in water and poppy seed. Refrigerate kabobs and sauce separately.   12 TO 16 SERVINGS.

Meat Kabobs

2 pounds pork tenderloin, cut into 1-inch
    pieces
2-pound frozen turkey roast, thawed and cut
    into 1-inch pieces
1 medium onion, finely chopped
½ cup soy sauce
¼ cup packed brown sugar
¼ cup lemon juice
1 teaspoon garlic salt
¾ to 1 teaspoon pepper
½ teaspoon ground coriander
⅛ teaspoon cayenne red pepper
    Dash of crushed red peppers

Place pork tenderloin pieces and turkey pieces in glass bowl. Mix remaining ingredients; pour on pork and turkey. Cover and refrigerate, stirring occasionally, 2 hours.

Set oven control to broil and/or 550°. Drain pork and turkey. Arrange pork and turkey on skewers. Place on rack in broiler pan. Broil 3 inches from heat until brown, about 8 minutes; turn. Broil 5 minutes.   12 TO 16 SERVINGS.

Ham Kabobs

Barbecue Sauce (below)
½ pound fully cooked ham, cut into cubes
1 medium zucchini, cut into ½-inch slices
1 cup cherry tomatoes
1 jar (5¼ ounces) cocktail onions, drained
1 cup pitted dates
1 can (8 ounces) pineapple chunks, drained

Prepare Barbecue Sauce. Your guests can thread remaining ingredients on bamboo skewers and brush them with Barbecue Sauce.　　6 SERVINGS.

BARBECUE SAUCE
Heat ½ cup chili sauce, 2 tablespoons brown sugar, 1½ teaspoons dry mustard and 1½ teaspoons prepared horseradish over medium heat until sugar is dissolved.

Snack Kabobs

Sweeteners (below)
1 pint strawberries
2 medium bananas, sliced
1 can (11 ounces) mandarin orange segments,
　　drained
4 ounces Cheddar, Fontina or Swiss cheese,
　　cut into ½-inch cubes

Prepare Sweeteners. Your guests can thread remaining ingredients on bamboo skewers and sprinkle or drizzle them with Sweeteners.　　6 SERVINGS.

SWEETENERS
Serve 2 or more of the following in bowls: ½ cup packed brown sugar, ½ cup orange-flavored liqueur, a mixture of ½ cup powdered sugar and ¼ teaspoon ground ginger.

To thread kabobs, place piece of beef on end of skewer.

Secure 1 end of bacon strip next to the piece of beef.

Add potato; bring the bacon around potato and secure.

If you like, garnish completed kabobs with green pepper.

Picnic-a-Bobs

Unseasoned meat tenderizer
1½-pound beef round steak, 1½ inches thick
½ cup red wine
⅓ cup vegetable oil
2 tablespoons lemon juice
2 cloves garlic, crushed
1 teaspoon salt
1 teaspoon dried dill weed
6 slices bacon
1 can (16 ounces) whole new potatoes, drained and cut in half

Apply tenderizer to beef round steak as directed on package. Cut beef into 18 pieces, about 1½x1 inch. Place in shallow glass or plastic dish. Mix wine, oil, lemon juice, garlic, salt and dill; pour on beef. Cover and refrigerate 2 hours, spooning marinade onto beef occasionally. Drain beef, reserving marinade.

Fry bacon until cooked but not crisp; drain. Thread a bacon slice alternately with beef and potato halves on each of 6 skewers as pictured.

Adjust charcoal grill so it is about 4 inches from hot coals. Your guests will enjoy grilling the assembled kabobs. Here's how:

Turn and baste kabobs with the reserved marinade until beef is done, about 15 minutes.   6 SERVINGS.

Mini Hot Dog Roast

1 large head red cabbage (about 3 pounds)
2 cans (about 2½ ounces each) cooking fuel
  Assorted relishes
  Mini Buns (right)
2 cans (8 ounces each) cocktail wieners

Cut cabbage in half; place each half cut side down on a tray. Hollow out center of each cabbage half; insert 1 can of cooking fuel in each hollow. Spear relishes with wooden picks; insert in base of cabbage halves. Prepare Mini Buns.

Heat wieners in boiling water 5 minutes; drain. Ignite cooking fuel. Your guests can toast their own wieners over the flaming cabbage. 6 TO 8 SERVINGS.

MINI BUNS

2¼ cups biscuit baking mix
½ cup shredded Cheddar cheese (about
   2 ounces)
½ cup cold water
 1 tablespoon prepared mustard
 1 tablespoon catsup
   Catsup
   Prepared mustard

Heat oven to 450°. Stir baking mix, cheese, water, 1 table-spoon mustard and 1 tablespoon catsup to a soft dough; beat vigorously 20 strokes. Gently smooth into a ball on floured cloth-covered board. Knead 5 times. Roll into rectangle, 14x10 inches, about ¼ inch thick. Cut into 2-inch squares.

Spread about ½ teaspoon catsup or mustard on half of each square; fold in half. Place on ungreased baking sheet. Bake until brown, 8 to 10 minutes. Serve warm.

After wieners are toasted, they are placed in buns.

Relishes are removed from base of cabbage halves.

Teriyaki Chicken Wings

3 to 3½ pounds chicken wings (about 20)
½ cup catsup
¼ cup dry white wine
¼ cup soy sauce
2 tablespoons sugar
1 teaspoon salt
½ teaspoon ground ginger
1 clove garlic, crushed

Cut ½ inch from tip of each chicken wing; separate at joint. Place chicken in ungreased baking dish, 13½x8¾x1¾ inches. Mix remaining ingredients; pour on chicken. Cover and refrigerate, turning chicken occasionally, at least 1 hour.

Heat oven to 375°. Remove chicken from baking dish, reserving sauce. Place chicken on rack in aluminum foil-lined broiler pan. Bake 30 minutes. Brush with reserved sauce. Turn chicken; bake, brushing occasionally with sauce, until chicken is glazed, 30 to 40 minutes.
8 TO 12 SERVINGS.

Chicken Bites

4 chicken breasts, boned, split and skin
  removed
1 cup finely crushed round buttery crackers
  (about 24)
½ cup grated Parmesan cheese
¼ cup finely chopped walnuts
½ teaspoon seasoned salt
1 teaspoon dried thyme leaves
1 teaspoon dried basil leaves
¼ teaspoon pepper
½ cup butter or margarine, melted

Cover 2 baking sheets with aluminum foil. Cut chicken into 1-inch pieces. Mix cracker crumbs, cheese, walnuts, seasoned salt, thyme, basil and pepper.

Heat oven to 400°. Dip chicken pieces into melted butter, then into crumb mixture. Place chicken pieces about ½ inch apart on baking sheets. Bake uncovered until golden brown, 20 to 25 minutes.   ABOUT 6 DOZEN APPETIZERS.

Drain the oysters and place on paper towels to dry.

Wrap each oyster with bacon slice; secure with pick.

Oysters Rumaki

12 slices bacon, cut in half
24 large fresh or frozen (thawed) oysters
½ teaspoon salt
¼ teaspoon pepper

Fry bacon 2 minutes on each side. Drain oysters; dry on paper towels. Sprinkle oysters with salt and pepper. Wrap each oyster with 1 bacon slice as pictured; secure with wooden pick. (At this point, rumakis can be covered and refrigerated up to 24 hours.) Heat oven to 400°. Place rumakis on rack in broiler pan. Bake 10 minutes; turn. Bake 10 minutes longer.   2 DOZEN APPETIZERS.

CREATIVE ACCESSORIES

When the mood of your party is casual and easygoing, throw the rule books away! Serve care-free but yummy food from your kitchen counter or make your coffee table your buffet and seat your friends on cushions around it, Eastern style. Use stack tables, plastic cubes, ottomans and pillows to create informal party areas. Set up a picnic table on the deck or even indoors. . .when it's all for fun, it's up to you.

Sauerkraut Surprises

1 cup sauerkraut, drained and cut up
1 package (3 ounces) sliced corned beef,
　　finely cut up (about 1 cup)
1 cup dry bread crumbs
1 egg, slightly beaten
1 small onion, finely chopped (about ¼ cup)
¼ cup water
2 tablespoons snipped parsley
1 teaspoon prepared horseradish
1 clove garlic, crushed
½ teaspoon salt
2 eggs, beaten
½ cup dry bread crumbs
　　Prepared mustard

Mix sauerkraut, corned beef, 1 cup bread crumbs, 1 egg, the onion, water, parsley, horseradish, garlic and salt; refrigerate at least 1 hour.

Heat oven to 400°. Shape sauerkraut mixture into 1-inch balls. Dip balls in 2 beaten eggs, then roll in ½ cup bread crumbs. Bake on ungreased baking sheet until light brown, about 20 minutes. Serve hot with mustard.　　2 TO 3 DOZEN APPETIZERS.

First dip the 1-inch sauerkraut balls in 2 beaten eggs.

Then roll balls in ½ cup dry bread crumbs and bake.

Do-Ahead Hot Cheese Puffs

    2 cups shredded sharp process cheese (about
        8 ounces)
 ½ cup butter or margarine, softened
    1 cup all-purpose flour*
    1 teaspoon freeze-dried chives
 ½ teaspoon seasoned salt

Mix cheese and butter; stir in flour, chives and seasoned
salt until blended. Shape into 1-inch balls; place on ungreased baking sheet. Cover and refrigerate up to 48 hours.

■**30 minutes before serving,** heat oven to 400°. Bake until
cheese puffs are set and light golden brown, 15 to 20
minutes.   ABOUT 3 DOZEN CHEESE PUFFS.

*If using self-rising flour, omit salt.

Place pimiento-stuffed olive or cheese slice on each to make Tip-Top Puffs.

Cover peanut, ham, bologna or olive half with dough to make filled puffs. Bake as directed.

Onion-Cheese Puffs

1 cup water
⅓ cup butter or margarine
1 cup all-purpose flour
1 teaspoon salt
¼ teaspoon garlic powder
4 eggs
¾ cup shredded Swiss or pizza cheese
   (about 3 ounces)
1 small Bermuda onion, chopped (about
   ¼ cup)

Heat oven to 400°. Heat water and butter to rolling boil. Stir in flour, salt and garlic powder. Stir vigorously over low heat 1 minute or until mixture forms a ball; remove from heat. Beat in eggs until smooth. Stir in cheese and onion. Drop dough by scant teaspoonfuls 1 inch apart onto lightly greased baking sheet. Bake until puffed and golden, 20 to 25 minutes.   ABOUT 6 DOZEN PUFFS.

Tip-Top Puffs: Place pimiento-stuffed olive or ½-inch-square cheese slice (⅛ inch thick) on each puff. Bake as directed.

Corn Bread Canapés

Corn Bread (below)
1 can (16 ounces) pork and beans, drained
2 green onions, chopped (about 2
   tablespoons)
2 tablespoons catsup
1 teaspoon Worcestershire sauce
½ teaspoon prepared mustard
¼ teaspoon liquid smoke
5 or 6 medium lettuce leaves
½ pound thinly sliced ham
8 slices American cheese

Bake Corn Bread. Mash pork and beans thoroughly. Stir in onions, catsup, Worcestershire sauce, mustard and liquid smoke. Spread over Corn Bread. Cut into 30 rectangles, about 2½x2 inches. Place on serving tray. Cut lettuce and ham slices into 30 rectangles each, about 2½x2 inches; layer on Corn Bread. Cut cheese with 1¾-inch canapé cutters or knife; place cheese cutouts on ham. Refrigerate until serving time.   2½ DOZEN CANAPES.

CORN BREAD

1 cup all-purpose flour*
1 cup yellow cornmeal
1 cup milk
¼ cup shortening
1 egg
2 tablespoons sugar
4 teaspoons baking powder
½ teaspoon salt

Heat oven to 400°. Grease jelly roll pan, 15½x10½x1 inch. Blend all ingredients about 20 seconds. Beat vigorously 1 minute. Pour into pan. Bake until golden brown, 10 to 12 minutes. Cool.

*If using self-rising flour, reduce baking powder to 2 teaspoons and omit salt.

Spread the bean mixture over cooled Corn Bread in pan.

Cut Corn Bread into rectangles; place on serving tray.

Layer the lettuce and ham rectangles on Corn Bread.

Cut the cheese with 1¾-inch canapé cutters or knife.

Stir cheese, bacon, peanuts and sliced green onions into the mayonnaise mixture.

Spread about 3 tablespoons of the bacon mixture over each slice of bread; bake.

Bacon Squares

- 1 cup mayonnaise or salad dressing
- 2 teaspoons Worcestershire sauce
- ½ teaspoon salad seasoning
- ¼ teaspoon paprika
- 2 cups shredded Cheddar cheese (about 8 ounces)
- 8 slices bacon, crisply fried and crumbled
- ⅓ cup chopped peanuts
- 4 green onions, sliced (about ¼ cup)
- 14 slices white bread

Heat oven to 400°. Mix mayonnaise, Worcestershire sauce, salad seasoning and paprika. Stir in cheese, bacon, peanuts and onions. Spread about 3 tablespoons bacon mixture over each slice of bread. Bake on ungreased baking sheet 10 minutes. Cut each slice into 4 pieces. Serve hot.

56 APPETIZERS.

Do-Ahead Mushroom Rounds

  6 slices white or whole wheat bread
  2 tablespoons butter or margarine, melted
 10 medium mushrooms, very finely chopped
      (about 1¼ cups)
  1 tablespoon butter or margarine
 ½ teaspoon garlic salt
  2 tablespoons cut-up pimiento, drained

Heat oven to 400°. Cut each bread slice into four 1½-inch circles; brush one side of bread circles with 2 tablespoons melted butter. Place buttered sides down on ungreased baking sheet. Bake bread circles until bottoms are light brown, about 5 minutes.

Cook and stir mushrooms in 1 tablespoon butter over low heat until mushrooms are brown, about 5 minutes. Stir in garlic salt. Spread about ½ teaspoon mushroom mixture on unbuttered side of each bread circle. Cover and refrigerate up to 24 hours.

■**15 minutes before serving,** heat oven to 350°. Garnish each round with small piece pimento. Bake about 4 minutes.
24 ROUNDS.

Cut each of the bread slices into four 1½-inch circles.

To save time, use two French knives to chop mushrooms.

Snack Thins

1 cup biscuit baking mix
½ cup shredded sharp Cheddar cheese
  (about 2 ounces)
¼ cup cold water
1½ teaspoons instant minced onion
1 can (5 ounces) Vienna sausages, drained

Heat oven to 400°. Stir baking mix, cheese, water and onion until a soft dough forms. Pat dough with floured hands or roll with floured rolling pin into oblong, 14x11 inches, on greased baking sheet, 15½x12 inches.

Cut each of 3 sausages lengthwise into 4 strips. Cut each of remaining 4 sausages crosswise into 6 slices. Press into dough. Bake until golden brown, 8 to 10 minutes. Cut into strips; serve warm.   6 SERVINGS.

BREAD-AND-BUTTER NOTE

When you're in a party mood, but your budget isn't, think about an easy, inexpensive bread-fest. You can bake or buy an assortment of crunchy, soft, sweet and sour breads in a variety of shapes and sizes. Serve them on boards accompanied by seasoned or flavored butters that you have molded ahead in fanciful butter molds or placed in butter crocks. If your budget can stretch, add cheese, cold meats, raw vegetables and fruits. It's old-fashioned and it's fun!

Avocado Sandwiches

1 medium avocado, pared and pitted
1 package (3 ounces) cream cheese, softened
1 teaspoon anchovy paste
1 teaspoon lemon juice
1 teaspoon onion juice
1 jar (2 ounces) broken pimiento-stuffed
   olives, chopped
21 slices day-old white sandwich bread

Mash avocado. Stir in cream cheese, anchovy paste, lemon juice, onion juice and olives. Trim crusts from bread; spread avocado mixture over bread. Cut each bread slice into 4 fingers or squares. Cover and refrigerate no longer than 2 hours. ABOUT 7 DOZEN SANDWICHES.

Cool Canapés

Beat ¼ cup butter or margarine, softened, 1 teaspoon finely shredded lemon peel, 1 tablespoon lemon juice, ½ teaspoon sugar and dash of red pepper sauce until fluffy. Cut 24 slices day-old white sandwich bread into circles with 2-inch biscuit cutter; spread butter mixture over bread circles. Cut 1 medium cucumber or zucchini into thin slices. Top each bread circle with cucumber slice; sprinkle with salt. ABOUT 4 DOZEN CANAPES.

An empty 14¼-ounce can is the right size for cutting the dough into 4-inch circles.

After placing circles on ungreased baking sheet, pinch edge of each to form a ridge.

Shrimp Mini Pizzas

2 packages active dry yeast
2 cups warm water (105 to 115°)
¼ cup vegetable oil
2 teaspoons sugar
2 teaspoons salt
4½ to 5¼ cups all-purpose flour*
1 can (15 ounces) tomato sauce
1½ teaspoons Italian seasoning
3 cans (4½ ounces each) small shrimp,
  drained
1 medium onion, chopped (about ½ cup)
¾ cup sliced ripe olives
½ large green pepper, chopped
1½ cups shredded mozzarella cheese (about
  6 ounces)
⅔ cup grated Parmesan cheese

Dissolve yeast in warm water in large bowl. Stir in oil, sugar, salt and 4 cups of the flour; beat until smooth. Turn dough onto floured surface. Knead in enough remaining flour to make dough easy to handle; knead until smooth, 3 to 5 minutes. Place in greased bowl; turn greased side up. Cover; let rise in warm place until double, about 45 minutes.

Heat oven to 400°. Mix tomato sauce and Italian seasoning. Punch down dough; divide in half. Roll each half into rectangle, 16x12 inches, on lightly floured surface. Cut each rectangle into twelve 4-inch circles; place circles on ungreased baking sheet. Pinch edge of each circle to form a ridge. Spoon 1 tablespoon of the tomato sauce mixture onto each pizza. Layer each pizza with remaining ingredients. (Pizzas can be prepared and refrigerated up to 3 hours before baking.) Bake until cheese is brown and bubbly, about 15 minutes.   2 DOZEN PIZZAS.

*If using self-rising flour, omit salt.

Spoon apple mixture diagonally onto each ham slice.

Roll each slice to form a cornucopia; fasten with pick.

Cornucopias

½ cup mayonnaise or salad dressing
1 tablespoon milk
½ teaspoon prepared horseradish
1 large apple, coarsely chopped
1 medium stalk celery, sliced (about ½ cup)
1 can (11 ounces) mandarin orange
   segments, drained
½ cup chopped walnuts
½ cup flaked coconut
8 to 10 slices cold boiled ham
   Parsley

Mix mayonnaise, milk and horseradish. Toss with remaining ingredients except ham and parsley. Spoon about ⅓ cup apple mixture diagonally onto each ham slice. Roll each slice to form a cornucopia; fasten with wooden pick. Serve over bed of parsley.   5 SERVINGS.

Crab Cakes—Southern Style

2 cans (7½ ounces each) crabmeat, drained
   and flaked
2 slices bread, torn into ¼-inch pieces
½ cup biscuit baking mix
½ cup mayonnaise or salad dressing
1 egg
½ teaspoon Worcestershire sauce
¼ teaspoon salt
⅛ teaspoon paprika
   Dash of ground nutmeg
⅓ cup biscuit baking mix
2 tablespoons butter or margarine
   Chili sauce or tartar sauce

Mix crabmeat, bread, ½ cup baking mix, the mayonnaise, egg, Worcestershire sauce, salt, paprika and nutmeg. Drop by ⅓ cupfuls into ⅓ cup baking mix, turning to coat on all sides. Shape into 2½-inch cakes.

Heat butter in 10-inch skillet over medium heat until melted. Fry cakes in butter until brown on both sides, 10 to 15 minutes. Serve with chili sauce.   8 OR 9 CAKES.

Mix the crabmeat, bread, ½ cup baking mix, the mayonnaise, egg and the seasonings.

After dropping mixture into baking mix, turn to coat on all sides. Shape into cakes; fry.

Divide dough into 6 equal parts; shape into balls.

After rising, roll each ball into a 6½-inch circle.

Place the circles on opposite corners of baking sheets.

Tear pocket bread in half or cut in half with scissors.

Gumbo-filled Pocket Bread

- 1 **package active dry yeast**
- 1⅓ **cups warm water (105 to 115°)**
- 1 **tablespoon vegetable oil**
- 1 **teaspoon salt**
- ¼ **teaspoon sugar**
- 1½ **cups whole wheat flour**
- 1½ **to 2 cups all-purpose flour***
   Cornmeal
   Gumbo Filling (right)

Dissolve yeast in warm water in large bowl; stir in oil, salt, sugar and whole wheat flour. Beat until smooth. Mix in enough all-purpose flour to make dough easy to handle. Knead on lightly floured surface until smooth and elastic, about 10 minutes. Place in greased bowl; turn greased side up. Cover and let rise in warm place until double, about 1 hour.

Punch down dough; divide into 6 parts. Shape each part into a ball. Cover and let rise 30 minutes. Sprinkle 3 ungreased baking sheets with cornmeal. Roll each ball into a 6½-inch circle on lightly floured surface. Place 2 circles on each baking sheet. Cover and let rise 30 minutes.

Heat oven to 450°. Bake circles until puffed and light brown, about 12 minutes. Tear in half and fill with Gumbo Filling.   6 POCKET BREADS.

*If using self-rising flour, omit salt.

GUMBO FILLING

Cook and stir 1½ pounds ground beef in 10-inch skillet until light brown; drain. Stir in 1 can (10¾ ounces) condensed chicken gumbo soup, ⅓ cup chili sauce, 2 tablespoons snipped parsley, 1 tablespoon instant minced onion and ½ teaspoon salt. Heat until mixture is hot.

Pour the catsup mixture on the beef and onion, then bake.

Cut thin diagonal slices across faces of cooled beef.

Beer Brisket Buns

- **3- pound corned beef brisket**
- **1 large Bermuda onion, sliced**
- **1 can (12 ounces) beer**
- **¾ cup catsup**
- **¼ cup barbecue sauce**
- **8 Kaiser rolls**

Heat oven to 325°. Place corned beef brisket on rack in baking pan, 9x9x2 inches. Roast uncovered 1 hour.

Remove rack from pan; drain. Place beef in pan and top with onion slices. Mix beer, catsup and barbecue sauce; pour on beef and onion. Bake uncovered until beef is tender, about 2 hours, spooning sauce onto beef and onion several times.

Cool beef in sauce. Cut thin diagonal slices across grain; heat beef and onion slices in sauce. Set oven control to broil and/or 550°. Split rolls and broil cut sides up 3 to 4 inches from heat until golden brown, about 1 minute. Serve hot beef and onion slices on rolls.   8 SERVINGS.

Hot Ham Sandwich Loaf

1 loaf (1 pound) unsliced whole wheat bread
¼ cup butter or margarine, softened
2 tablespoons snipped chives
1 tablespoon prepared mustard
16 slices chopped ham luncheon meat
16 slices Swiss cheese
2 tablespoons butter or margarine, melted
1 tablespoon poppy seed

Heat oven to 400°. Make 8 diagonal cuts from top almost through to bottom of loaf.

Mix ¼ cup butter, the chives and mustard. Spread 1 side of each slice with butter mixture. Place loaf on piece of aluminum foil, 20x18 inches. Alternate 2 ham slices and 2 cheese slices in each cut. Brush loaf with 2 tablespoons butter; sprinkle with poppy seed. Wrap securely in foil. (At this point, loaf can be refrigerated up to 24 hours.) Bake on ungreased baking sheet 30 minutes.   8 SERVINGS.

Make diagonal cuts almost through to bottom of loaf.

Alternate 2 ham slices and 2 cheese slices in each cut.

Cut through sauerkraut with kitchen scissors; add corned beef, cheese and mayonnaise.

Spread about ⅓ cup of the sauerkraut mixture onto each slice of toast; bake 10 minutes.

Open-Face Reubens

14 slices dark rye bread, toasted
   Prepared mustard
 1 can (16 ounces) sauerkraut, drained
 2 packages (3 ounces each) sliced corned
   beef, finely snipped
 2 cups shredded pizza or Swiss cheese
   (about 8 ounces)
½ cup mayonnaise or salad dressing

Heat oven to 375°. Spread toast lightly with mustard; place on ungreased baking sheet. Cut through sauerkraut with scissors. Stir in corned beef, cheese and mayonnaise.

Spread about ⅓ cup sauerkraut mixture onto each slice of toast. Bake until sauerkraut mixture is hot and cheese is melted, about 10 minutes. Cut sandwiches in half.

28 OPEN-FACE SANDWICHES.

SANDWICH SAVVY

1. Choose interesting breads and colorful fillings. For color as well as taste, combine two kinds of bread in one sandwich.

2. Bland fillings can be pepped up with lemon juice, mustard or sauces. Crunchiness can be added with bacon bits, nuts, cucumber or celery; color with chopped pickles, pimiento, green pepper or parsley garnishes.

3. One way to keep sandwiches fresh is to place a damp towel in the bottom of a large shallow pan with edges of towel hanging over the sides. Cover with waxed paper. Stack sandwiches with waxed paper between layers and on top. Fold the edges of the towel snugly over the sandwiches.

Circle Hot Dogs

8 skinless frankfurters
2 small tomatoes, each cut into 4 slices
8 slices process American cheese
4 hamburger buns, split and toasted
8 pickle slices

Make cuts almost to bottom of frankfurters; place in ungreased baking pan. Place a tomato slice and a cheese slice on each bun half; place on ungreased baking sheet.

Set oven control to broil and/or 550°. Broil frankfurters with tops 4 to 5 inches from heat until brown and curled, 2 to 3 minutes. Place frankfurters on cheese-topped buns. Broil until cheese is melted, 3 to 4 minutes. Garnish with pickle slices.   4 TO 6 SERVINGS.

Toast bun halves with tops 4 to 5 inches from heat.

Make diagonal cuts almost to bottom of franks; broil.

Place tomato slice and cheese slice on each bun half.

Place broiled frankfurters on buns; broil about 3 minutes.

Mix mayonnaise and mustard; spread over bread slices.

Top half of slices with lettuce, beef, pickles and tomatoes.

Stag Sandwich

⅓ cup mayonnaise or salad dressing
2 teaspoons prepared mustard
10 slices rye bread
   Lettuce leaves
1 can (12 ounces) corned beef, cut into
   10 thin slices
2 medium garlic dill pickles, thinly sliced
2 medium tomatoes, sliced and salted
   Potato chips

Mix mayonnaise and mustard; spread over bread slices. Top half of the slices with lettuce, corned beef, pickles and tomato slices. Cover with remaining bread slices. Serve with potato chips.　5 SERVINGS.

Danish Smørrebrød

SHRIMP SANDWICH

For each sandwich, cover 1 buttered bread slice (see note) with a lettuce leaf. Arrange 1 to 2 tablespoons tiny shrimp, drained, on center of lettuce. Arrange hard-cooked egg slices and cherry tomato slices on either side of shrimp. Sprinkle with dried dill weed.

HAM AND EGG SANDWICH

For each sandwich, place 1 thin slice fully cooked ham on half of 1 buttered bread slice. Arrange hard-cooked egg slices on other half. Sprinkle with sliced green onion.

BEEF AND GHERKIN SANDWICH

For each sandwich, place 1 thin slice roast beef on 1 buttered bread slice. Top with sliced dill gherkin pickles, onion slices and sieved egg yolk.

BEEF AND HERRING SANDWICH

For each sandwich, place 2 thin slices roast beef on half of 1 buttered bread slice. Place 3 to 5 pieces pickled herring, well drained, on remaining half. Top with cherry tomato slices, cucumber slices and snipped parsley.

SARDINE SANDWICH

For each sandwich, place 3 to 5 sardines, well drained, on half of 1 buttered bread slice. Place 1 to 2 tablespoons scrambled egg on remaining half. Top with shredded Cheddar cheese and sliced green onion.

Note: Spread soft butter or margarine to edges of thinly sliced rye or whole wheat bread to prevent sandwiches from becoming dry or soaked by sandwich ingredients.

Spread soft butter or margarine to the edges of bread.

Arrange ingredients in rows, overlapping when necessary.

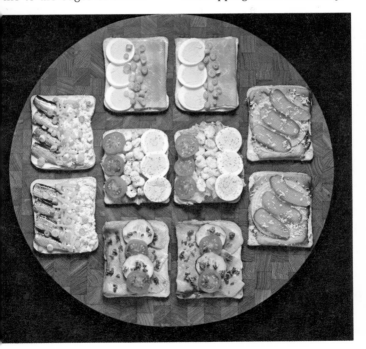

Shrimp-wiches

½ loaf (1-pound size) French bread
2 cans (4¾ ounces each) chicken spread
2 tablespoons mayonnaise or salad dressing
½ teaspoon poultry seasoning
1 cup shredded Muenster cheese (4 ounces)
  Leaf lettuce
  Mayonnaise or salad dressing
1 medium cucumber, thinly sliced
1 medium tomato, sliced
1 can (4½ ounces) tiny shrimp, rinsed and drained
3 tablespoons mayonnaise or salad dressing
  Grated Parmesan cheese

Cut loaf lengthwise in half; place halves cut sides up. Mix chicken spread, 2 tablespoons mayonnaise and the poultry seasoning; spread over bread halves. Top with Muenster cheese, lettuce, mayonnaise, cucumber and tomato slices. Cut each half into thirds. Mix shrimp and 3 tablespoons mayonnaise; spoon onto each sandwich. Sprinkle with Parmesan cheese.   6 OPEN-FACE SANDWICHES.